RACE TO THE NORTH POLE: PEARY VS. COOK

CONTENTS

Written by Anita Ganeri

Collins

1 AN AMAZING FEAT

On the morning of 7th September 1909, people in the USA woke up to sensational news. Splashed across the front of the *New York Times* newspaper was the headline:

[...]w York Times.

THE WEATHER.

Fair, warmer to-day; clouding to-morrow; light, variable winds.

[...]DAY, SEPTEMBER 7, 1909.—EIGHTEEN PAGES.

ONE CENT In Greater New York, Jersey City, and Newark { Elsewhere, TWO CENTS.

PEARY DISCOVERS THE NORTH POLE AFTER EIGHT TRIALS IN 23 YEARS

In order not to miss The New York Times of to-morrow, in which will be printed exclusively Lieut. Peary's own story of his discovery of the North Pole, order a copy from your newsdealer early to-day.

COOK GLAD PEARY REACHED THE POLE

Unmoved When, Wreathed with Flowers at Banquet, He Hears the News.

HOPE NOW FOR OTHERS

Believes More Expeditions Will Reach the Pole Within the Next Ten Years.

COPENHAGEN, Sept. 6.—Copenhagen was electrified to-night by the report of Commander Peary's announcement that he had reached the north pole. Dr. Cook was immensely interested and said:

"That is good news. I hope Peary did get to the pole. His observations, and reports on that region will confirm mine."

Asked if there was any probability of Peary's having found the tube containing his records, Dr. Cook replied:

"I hope so, but that is doubtful on account of the drift. Commander Peary would [illegible] pole this year, [illegible] last year. [illegible] hundred miles east of [illegible] are rivals, of course, but the [illegible] good enough for two.

"The fact of two men having reached [...]

Notifies The New York Times That He Reached It on April 6, 1909.

HE WIRES FROM LABRADOR

Returning on the Roosevelt, Which He Reports to Bridgman Is Safe.

IS NEARING NEWFOUNDLAND

Expects to Reach Chateau Bay To-day, When He Will Send Full Particulars.

McMILLAN SENDS WORD

Explorer's Companion Telegraphs Sister: "We Have the Pole on Board."

SEVEN VAIN EXPEDITIONS

Many Years Consumed in Learning the Feasible Route—Picked Men Were His Assistants.

Commander Robert E. Peary, U. S. [...] has discovered the north pole. Fol-[...]

PEARY REPORTS TO THE TIMES

ANNOUNCES HIS DISCOVERY OF THE POLE AND WILL SEND A FULL AND EXCLUSIVE ACCOUNT TO-DAY.

Indian Harbor, Labrador, via Cape Ray, N. F., Sept. 6.

The New York Times, New York:

I have the pole, April sixth. Expect arrive Chateau Bay September seventh. Secure control wire for me there and arrange expedite transmission big story.

PEARY.

PEARY'S MESSAGE TO HIS WIFE.

SOUTH HARPSWELL, Me., Sept. 6.—Commander Robert E. Peary announced his success in discovering the North Pole to his wife, who is summering at Eagle Island here, as follows:

INDIAN HARBOR, via Cape Ray, Sept. 6, 1909.

Mrs. R. E. Peary, South Harpswell, Me.:

Have made good at last. I have the old Pole. Am well. Love. Will wire again from Chateau.

(Signed) BERT.

In [illegible] Mrs. Peary sent the following dispatch:

SOUTH HARPSWELL, Me., Sept. 6, 1909.

To Commander R. E. Peary, Steamer Roosevelt, Chateau Bay:

All well. Best love. God bless you. Hurry home.

(Signed) JO.

On 6th April, the article said, Commander Robert E Peary of the US Navy had become the first person to reach the North Pole. He had sent a message to the paper, proudly informing it of his record-breaking feat.

As the news spread around the world, congratulations poured in for Peary. It was a dream come true and he was thrilled with his new-found fame. Of course, it hadn't been easy going. In total, he'd spent 23 gruelling years in the Arctic, trying to achieve his goal. He'd been stuck in ice, almost starved to death, and lost most of his toes to **frostbite**. But it had all been worth it – he'd earned his place in history, and no one could take that away.

Readers were gripped by Peary's death-defying adventures. At that time, the North Pole was still one of the most mysterious places on Earth. Most people didn't really know what or where it was and couldn't imagine why it had been so tricky to find.

If you're planning on following in Peary's footsteps, here's a *VERY* IMPORTANT TRAVEL TIP.

VERY IMPORTANT TRAVEL TIP

Make sure you pick the right North Pole.
There are three to choose from:

1. *Geographic North Pole*: the most northerly point on Earth, at the northern end of Earth's **axis**. It's about 725 kilometres north of Greenland in the middle of the Arctic Ocean. Most of the time, it's covered in sea ice.
2. ***Magnetic** North Pole*: where Earth's **magnetic field** is strongest, and where you'll end up if you follow the arrow "north" on your compass. It's hundreds of kilometres south of the Geographic North Pole and shifts its position day by day.
3. ***Geomagnetic** North Pole*: the northern end of Earth's magnetic field. It's not a precise point but stretches a few kilometres across Earth. It is also constantly changing location.

1
2
3

North Pole Visitors' Guide

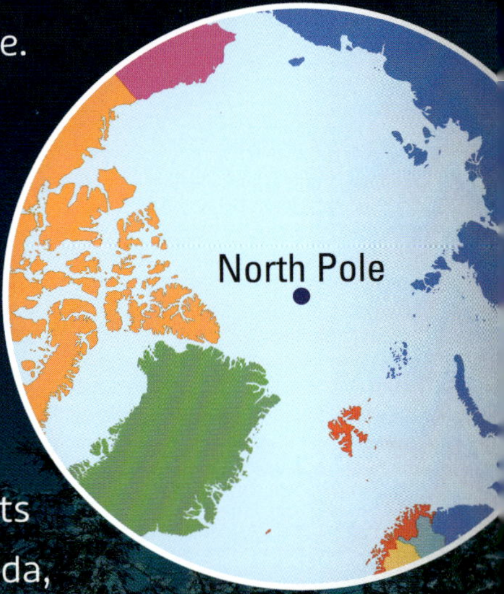

- There's no land at the North Pole. It's located in the middle of the Arctic Ocean.
- Parts of the Arctic Ocean are permanently frozen. Others usually freeze in winter but melt again in spring.
- The ocean and the northern parts of the countries around it (Canada, the USA, Greenland, Norway and Russia) are known as the Arctic.

North Pole

- The name "Arctic" comes from the ancient Greek word "arktos" which means "bear". Greek explorers called the Arctic "the land under the constellation of the Great Bear".

Arctic Weather Report

Arctic winters are long and bitterly cold, with temperatures falling as low as –68 degrees Celsius. The sun doesn't rise for months on end, so it's dark all day and all night. Summers are shorter but much warmer, with temperatures rising as high as 10 degrees Celsius. There is 24-hour daylight because the Sun doesn't set for months on end.

Before Peary, many expeditions had set off for the Arctic. Some were searching for new trade routes. Some were hunting for seals and whales. Some were made up of scientists, keen to study the unusual landscape and wildlife. Others simply wanted to get there first. Whatever their reasons, many of these intrepid explorers ended up lost, ill or dead.

Even some of the greatest explorers failed to reach the North Pole.

Name: Fridtjof Nansen

Born: 1861

Died: 1930

Nationality: Norwegian

In 1893, Fridtjof Nansen set out from Oslo in his ship, *Fram*. He planned to sail into the Arctic Ocean, then **drift** with the ice and ocean currents towards the Pole. At first, everything worked perfectly, even though progress was seriously slow. The ship drifted for almost two years, and finally Nansen decided to set off on foot. He broke the record for reaching the furthest north but had to turn back before the North Pole.

So, how did Peary reach the North Pole when so many others had failed? Well, it all goes back to his childhood ...

2 EXPLORER IN TRAINING

Robert Edwin Peary was born in the USA, on 6th May 1856. When he was only two years old, his father died and he was brought up by his mother who spoilt him rotten.

Young Robert found it difficult to make friends even though he longed to be liked. This carried on through his whole life. It didn't help that his favourite hobby was **taxidermy**. He often spent hours going for long walks on his own, in the woods along the coast, searching for dead animals to work on.

Then, one day, his life changed forever. He read a brilliant book about the Arctic and, from then on, all he wanted was to be a famous Arctic explorer.

Cape Elizabeth, where Peary grew up and would hunt for dead animals

After college, Peary joined the US Navy as an engineer. He was sent to Central America to find a route through the rainforests for a new canal. He loved being outside all day, in the wild, and hated having to go back to the USA and his desk. So, he read everything he could about the Arctic, and began making plans to go there himself.

modern Qeqertarsuaq, where Peary first landed in Greenland in 1886

In 1886, Peary borrowed some money from his mother and took six months' leave from his job. Then, he set off on his first Arctic expedition – to the ice-capped island of Greenland. After several weeks, he ran low on food and, reluctantly, turned back.

As soon as he got home, he set to work organising another expedition – to make the first crossing of the ice cap itself. But, before he could even set off, news came that Nansen had beaten him to it. This didn't stop Peary; he simply changed his route.

While most explorers stuck to the coast, Peary planned to head north and inland. His new route was so risky, it didn't appear on any map.

Joining Peary on the trip was Matthew Henson, an African-American explorer who'd met Peary while working in a hat shop. Before that, he'd spent years sailing the world after running away to sea at the age of 12. As Peary's most trusted assistant, he often saved the day.

The expedition sailed from New York City on 6th June 1891, but before long, disaster struck. While the ship, the *SS Kite*, was crashing its way through the ice on Baffin Bay, Peary broke his leg in a freak accident. At the nearest land, he was carried ashore. The ship's doctor, Frederick Cook, managed to **set** his leg, but Peary was forced to spend the next six months recovering.

looking out across the frozen Baffin Bay

Peary was a terrible patient. He hated having to rest and kept himself busy by making preparations for the difficult journey ahead. He sent Henson and some of the other men to visit the local Inuit. They'd lived around the North Pole for centuries and were experts at Arctic survival. Peary knew he'd need their knowledge and skills if he wanted to come back alive.

From the Inuit, Peary's men learnt how to make warm clothes from animal skins, build igloos and drive dog sleds.

Henson was a very fast learner, mastering sled driving and hunting. He got on very well with the Inuit and was fascinated by their culture. He was even learning to speak the Inuit language fluently.

Matthew Henson

Finally, on 3rd May 1892, Dr Cook declared Peary well enough to get going again. Peary couldn't wait, but the journey across the ice was horribly slow. On the way, one of the sleds broke down and some of the dogs fell ill and died. Deep snow blocked the way and they were held up for three days by **blizzards**.

The people back at base camp were getting worried. For weeks they'd had no news, and very soon the ship would arrive to take the expedition home. If they wanted to leave the Arctic safely, before winter, time was running out. Was Peary alive or dead? They couldn't wait much longer to find out.

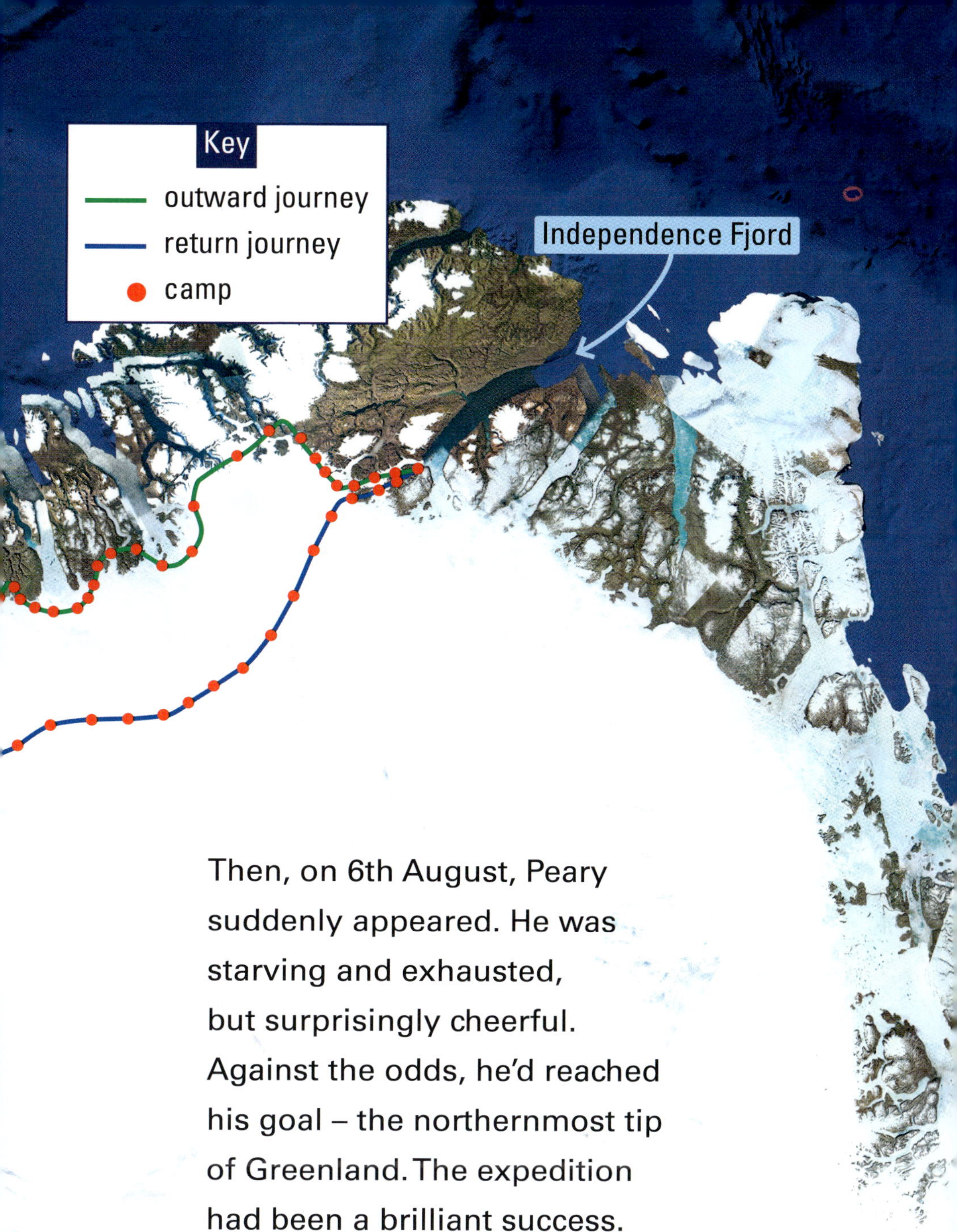

Then, on 6th August, Peary suddenly appeared. He was starving and exhausted, but surprisingly cheerful. Against the odds, he'd reached his goal – the northernmost tip of Greenland. The expedition had been a brilliant success.

3 DREAMS OF THE POLE

A year later, Peary was back in Greenland, but the expedition ended in disaster when almost all of the sled dogs died. Even then, Peary wasn't put off. In 1898, he set off again, this time for the North Pole. He had five years' leave from the Navy, and the backing of the **prestigious** Peary Arctic Club which had been set up in his honour.

Peary's camp on Ellesmere Island

Peary was desperate to get going. But winter was coming, and his ship was no match for the thick Arctic ice. Soon, it was well and truly stuck. It was still more than 320 kilometres short of base camp.

But Peary refused to give up. Taking a massive risk, he decided to set out for base camp by sled. By now, it was freezing cold and dark for weeks on end. By the time he reached base camp, his feet were so badly frostbitten, he lost most of his toes.

Back in the USA, the Peary Arctic Club was shocked by the news and immediately sent a ship to bring Peary home. Once again, Dr Frederick Cook was on board. But Peary stubbornly refused any help. Then, unbelievably, he set out for the North Pole again.

Robert Peary and his wife Josephine

Here's what he might have written in a letter to his wife, Jo:

The Arctic, 1899

My dearest Jo,

I set off for the Pole with Henson and some of the Inuit. We reckoned it was around 650 kilometres away, which didn't sound too bad, but the ice kept cracking under our feet. As for the blizzards ... after two weeks, we were still well short of our goal. None of us could go any further – my feet are wrecked. Another failure, I'm afraid, but I'm not giving up.

Your husband,

Robert

Peary was soon planning his *next* trip north. Fortunately, he now had plenty of backers, including the US president himself.

This time, he had a ship specially built to cope with the ice. He named it *SS Roosevelt*, after the president. The ship did its job brilliantly. By September 1905, Peary had reached his camp at the edge of the Arctic Ocean. He was exactly where he wanted to be.

SS Roosevelt

Robert Peary aboard *SS Roosevelt* with some sled dogs

From then on, however, things quickly went downhill. Shortly after the team set off for the Pole, they were stopped in their tracks by a huge stretch of open water. It took a week for the water to freeze over enough for them to get across. Almost immediately, a blizzard blew up and beat them back, and later on, they almost starved to death.

So, Peary didn't reach the North Pole. But he did manage to keep his backers happy by naming features along the coast after them!

4 THIRD TIME LUCKY?

On 6th July 1908, Peary sailed once again from New York in *SS Roosevelt*. It had taken more than a year to repair the ship after its last voyage. This would be his eighth trip to the Arctic and his third and final attempt to reach the North Pole.

He'd hand-picked a top team for the trip. Among them were …

1908 North Pole expedition

Robert Peary – expedition leader

Matthew Henson – Peary's assistant and second-in-command

Robert Bartlett – master of *SS Roosevelt*

George Wardwell – chief engineer

John Murphy – **boatswain**

Professor Ross Gilmore Marvin – chief scientist

Donald Baxter MacMillan – teacher and explorer

Dr John Goodsell – surgeon and ship's doctor

George Borup – **geologist** and explorer

expedition members pictured on a sled

Sailing up Baffin Bay, Peary headed for a settlement on Etah on the northwest coast of Greenland. Here, he hired the best local Inuit sled-drivers and dogs, and stocked up on whale and walrus meat.

From there, he sailed to Cape Sheridan on nearby Ellesmere Island, where the ship spent the winter. Immediately, men were sent out to take food and other supplies to base camp, about 150 kilometres to the west.

Peary kept his team busy over the long, dark winter. There were sleds to make, fur clothes to sew, and rations to work out. There were also plenty of Arctic hares to hunt so they had fresh meat to eat.

By the following spring, everything was in place ...

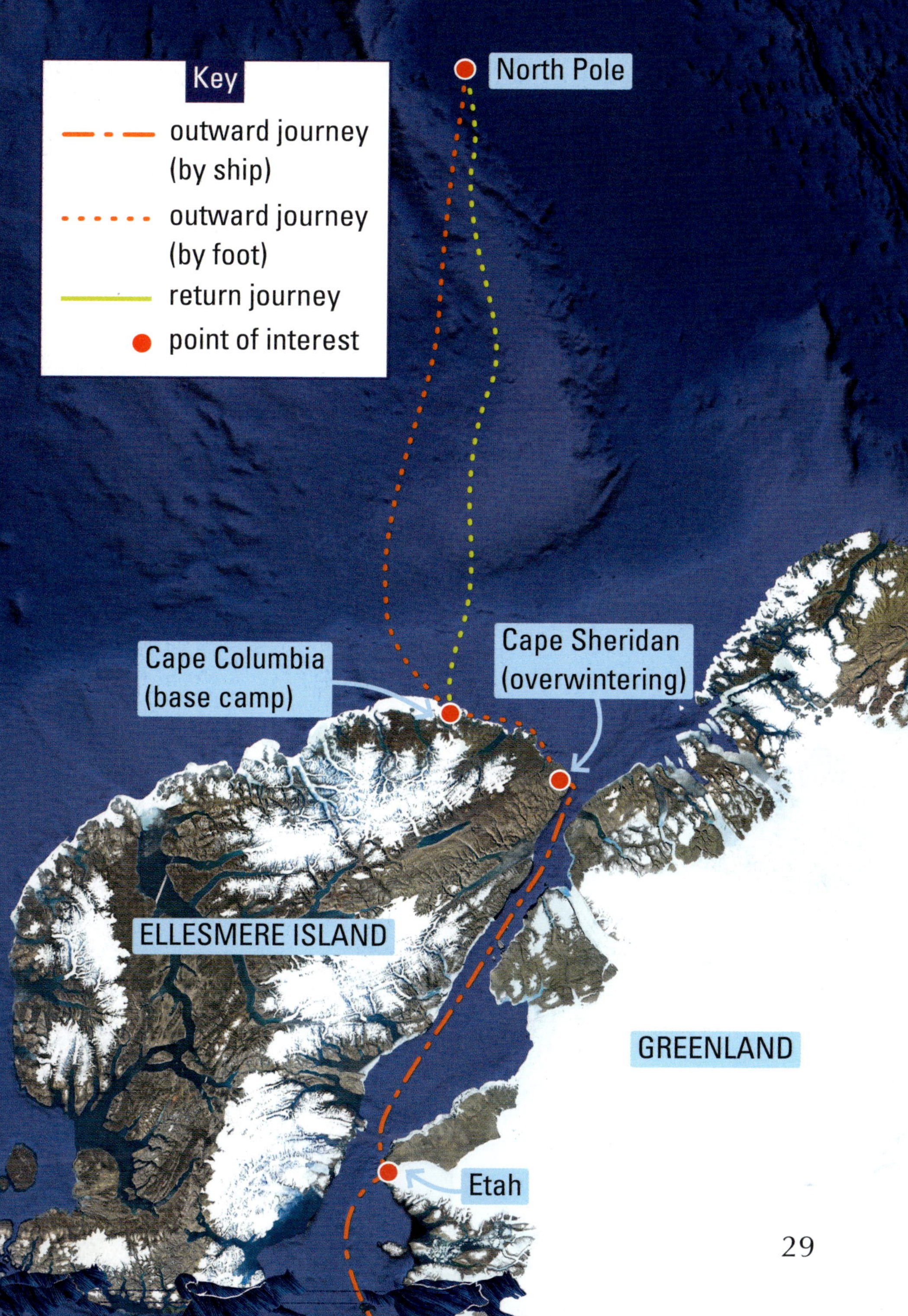
Key
outward journey (by ship)
outward journey (by foot)
return journey
point of interest
North Pole
Cape Columbia (base camp)
Cape Sheridan (overwintering)
ELLESMERE ISLAND
GREENLAND
Etah

1st March 1909

Peary leads 24 men, 19 sleds and 133 dogs from base camp onto the frozen ocean. Bartlett skis ahead to warn of danger. Peary brings up the rear.

Bartlett and his sled party

A few days later

The warm weather brings the risk of the ice melting. Once again, they're held up for days when a huge stretch of water opens up.

Peary's team crossing ice and water

14th March

Fuel and food are running low, but there's been no sign of the sled bringing fresh supplies. It finally catches up with them, to Peary's great relief.

26th March

The weather's colder now and the ice easier to cross. One by one, the sleds bringing supplies for the return journey are sent back to base.

Matthew Henson

2nd April

Peary chooses six men for the final push – himself, Henson and four of the Inuit. It's now just over 200 kilometres to the North Pole. Will it be third time lucky?

North Pole diary

By Robert E Peary

6th April 1909

We're here. We're here at last.

I've reached the North Pole!

I can't believe I'm actually here. The ice was smooth and hard, and the dogs able to speed along. We were exhausted, starving and I don't know how we kept going. However, at 10 o'clock this morning, we reached the North Pole. Finally.

I took readings with the **sextant** to check our position. It might not be the exact spot, but we're close enough.

What Peary might have written ...

Then, we planted the American flag in the ice, posed for some photos, and left a message to say we were claiming the North Pole for the USA. This is truly the proudest day of my life.

But Peary was in for a shock ...

5 COOK AND CONTROVERSY

While Peary was making his way back from the North Pole, another explorer was causing a stir. Dr Frederick Cook was guest of honour at a grand **banquet** in Copenhagen, Denmark, where he was celebrating *his* discovery of the North Pole on 21st April 1908.

Peary knew Cook was planning something, but he hadn't taken it seriously. He was far too busy with his own preparations to worry about it too much. Now, though, Cook was claiming to have reached the North Pole a *whole year* before him. It was unbelievable.

Peary was furious. He already knew Cook, of course, from their earlier expeditions together, but they were very different. Peary was tough and tricky to get along with. Cook was likeable and easy-going. Despite this, they'd liked and respected each other, but all that was about to change.

Dr Frederick Cook arriving to a hero's welcome in Copenhagen

Cook had initially set his sights on Antarctica, at the other end of the world. In 1898, he joined a Belgian expedition as ship's surgeon. When the ship became stuck fast in the ice, Cook helped save the day. He came up with a plan to free the ship, by sawing a long **channel** through the ice to the open water.

Always kind and cheerful, Cook worked hard to keep the crew's spirits up through the winter. He also proved handy at hunting penguins. As a doctor, he realised the men needed fresh meat to help stop **scurvy**.

Back in Belgium, Cook was treated like a hero, and was given many medals and awards.

Belgica's crew

Ship's mate
Among the ship's crew was Norwegian, Roald Amundsen. He later became the first person to reach the South Pole and is one of the greatest explorers of all time.
the Belgica

In 1906, Cook led a daring expedition to Denali, the highest mountain in North America at 6,190 metres. Despite having no climbing experience, he claimed to have reached the top on 16th September – the first person ever to do so.

faked photo of Cook on Denali summit

It might have sounded too good to be true, but Cook was now a hero in the USA, too. As the only American to have explored both ends of Earth, he was elected President of the Explorers' Club of New York. It was a great honour. All in all, it now seemed the perfect time to race Peary to the North Pole.

Cook soon found a suitable ship and loaded it with two years' worth of supplies in case it got stuck in the ice. He kept his plans top secret, until he was well on his way. If anyone asked what he was doing, he said he was off on a long hunting trip.

By 3rd July 1907, he was ready to sail for Greenland.

Denali today

From Greenland, Cook planned to travel west, cross Ellesmere Island, then head north over the **pack ice** to the Pole. He and his team left Greenland in February 1908. By August, they had still not returned. Winter was coming and they were running out of food. Surely, by now, they must be dead?

members of the Cook expedition to the North Pole, 1908

Then, on 18th April 1909, three wild-looking figures stumbled into camp. They were filthy, and starving, with long, matted hair and beards. Cook claimed they'd survived against the odds and reached the North Pole almost a year before, on 21st April 1908.

Here's how the extraordinary story of his journey might have gone …

Frederick Cook

Around 800 kilometres of pack ice lay between us and the Pole. At first, we made steady progress, but danger was never far away. In places, the ice was so thin, it cracked under our feet. One night, it gave way under my tent and I fell into the freezing sea. Happily, my reindeer-skin sleeping bag kept me dry.

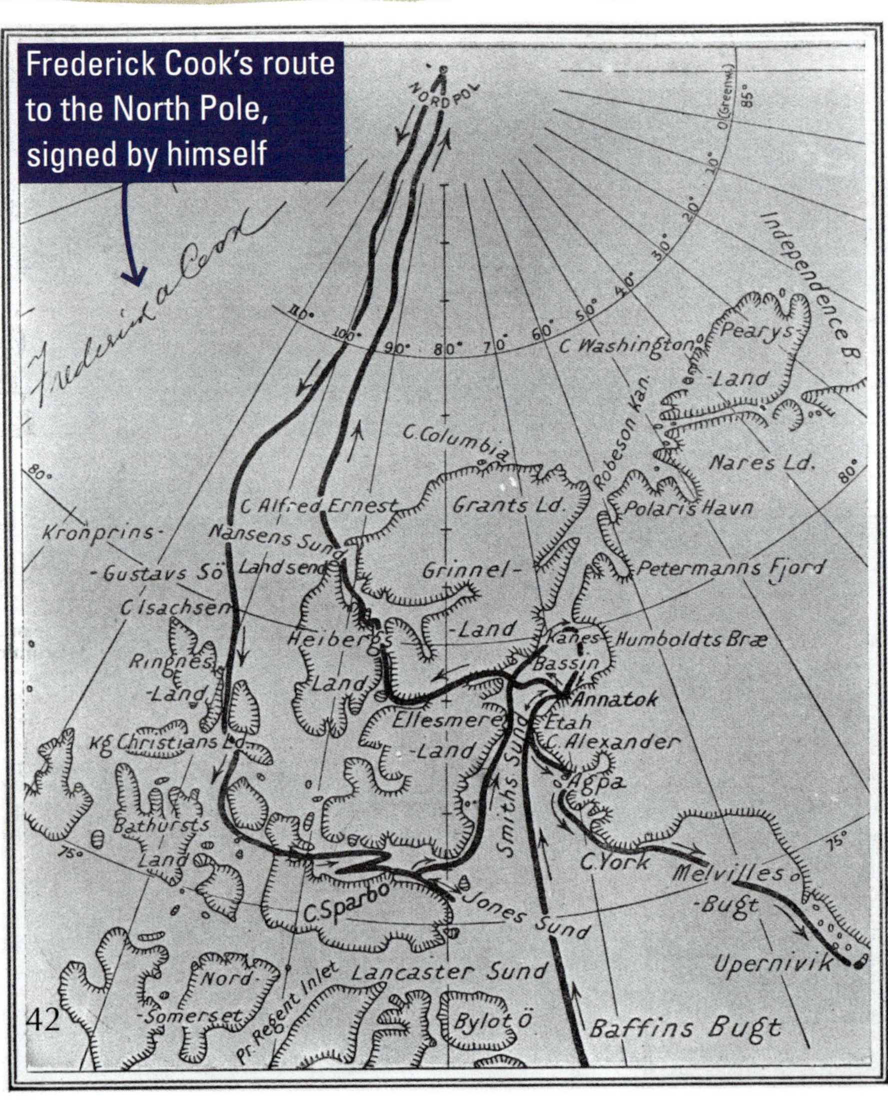

Frederick Cook's route to the North Pole, signed by himself

We reached the North Pole on 21st April 1908. We hoped to come back the way we went, but we'd drifted way off course. Winter was coming and our food was running low. The only option was to sail for land in our collapsable canvas boat.

What a dreadful journey. The boat was cut to shreds by ice and walrus tusks. We kept patching it up with bits of boot leather, but they didn't hold for long. We were so glad to spot an island and spent the winter there in a cave.

When spring came, we began the long trek back to base camp. Luckily, we hadn't used up all our boot leather – it was all we had to eat on the way.

Taken by Cook, this photograph shows his two companions, at the North Pole on 21st April 1908.

6 IT'S STILL A MYSTERY

Cook arriving back in the USA in 1909

Cook was desperate to get home as quickly as possible and tell the world about his amazing achievement. After a long sled journey, he found a place on a Danish whaling ship. In his rush, he left his papers and instruments behind in the Arctic with instructions for one of his team to bring them back once they'd packed up the camp. When Peary found out about this, on his own way back from the Pole, he gave orders for them to be buried under a pile of rocks.

For centuries, explorers had failed to find the North Pole. Now, *two* Americans were claiming to have reached it. But who was telling the truth?

At first, the public took Cook's side. On his return to the USA, cheering crowds greeted him with "WE BELIEVE IN YOU!" banners. Meanwhile, Peary was accused of being a bad loser for calling Cook a cheat.

a banner welcoming Frederick Cook back to New York City

Peary and Cook now had to prove themselves. They were asked to hand over their expedition papers and photographs to be checked by top scientists. But even these experts found it hard to agree …

Finally, the scientists reached their verdict. It was official – Peary had reached the North Pole first. Cook was guilty of cheating – there was no proof he'd ever got that far.

Le Petit Journal

ADMINISTRATION
61, RUE LAFAYETTE, 61
Les manuscrits ne sont pas rendus
On s'abonne sans frais dans tous les bureaux de poste

5 CENT. SUPPLÉMENT ILLUSTRÉ 5 CENT.

20me Année — Numéro 983
DIMANCHE 19 SEPTEMBRE 1909

ABONNEMENTS
SEINE et SEINE-ET-OISE.. 2 fr.
DÉPARTEMENTS.......... 2 fr.
ÉTRANGER 2 50

LA CONQUÊTE DU POLE NORD
Le docteur Cook et le commandant Peary s'en disputent la

Cook still insisted he was telling the truth. He travelled around Europe and the USA, giving lectures about his trip. Many people came to the lectures – some out of curiosity, some to throw eggs at him.

Meanwhile, Peary couldn't have been happier. After the verdict, he set off on a victory tour of Europe. But there were still plenty of people who thought Peary wasn't being totally honest and had something to hide. Peary died in 1920 but his claim to have reached the North Pole first is still being argued over today.

a poster advertising Peary's lecture tour

the monument erected to Robert Peary in Greenland

Robert Peary's grave

Henry Coxwell's 1880 idea for hydrogen-filled balloons to travel to the North Pole

Since Peary, many explorers from around the world have reached the North Pole – by sled, hot-air balloon, airship, plane, ship, submarine and on foot.

On 6th April 1969, British explorer Wally Herbert reached the North Pole. The 5,600-kilometre journey took him nearly 14 months. If Peary's claim was false, this made Herbert the first to reach the Pole by foot. The only person to have got there before him was Russian, Aleksandr Kuznetsov, who flew there by plane on 23rd April 1948.

In 2005, another British explorer, Tom Avery, set out to retrace Peary's actual route to the Pole. He wanted to prove Peary's journey could be done in the time he claimed. Using **replica** sleds and equipment, Avery beat Peary's time by five hours. This may have been due to different ice conditions, or perhaps it proved Peary right.

We'll probably never know for certain who reached the North Pole first. But perhaps it doesn't matter. Both Peary and Cook, and every member of their various expeditions, showed enormous bravery in attempting to conquer the Arctic in the first place.

GLOSSARY

axis an imaginary straight line that runs down the middle of Earth from the North Pole to the South Pole – Earth spins around on its axis

banquet a large, formal meal for lots of people

blizzards severe storms with very strong winds that whip up the snow so that it is difficult to see

boatswain a sailor who looks after the ship and its equipment

channel a long stretch of water

drift be carried by the movement of the water

frostbite an injury caused by extreme cold, usually affecting a person's fingers, toes, ears or nose

geologist an expert in Earth's structure, including rocks and fossils

geomagnetic relating to Earth's magnetic field

magnetic to do with magnets and how they work

magnetic field the area around a magnet that attracts objects to itself – Earth acts like a giant magnet and has its own magnetic field

pack ice a large stretch of ice floating in the sea that has been formed by smaller pieces being pushed and forced together

prestigious important and admired

replica an exact copy of an object

scurvy an illness that is caused by not having enough Vitamin C in your body – it was common among sailors on long voyages

set to put a broken bone back in its correct place

sextant an instrument used for measuring angles between the sun and Earth for discovering your exact location

taxidermy a way of collecting, preparing and stuffing animal skins so that they look like a model of the real animal and can be put on display

INDEX

COOK OR PEARY?

So, who do you think reached the North Pole first – Cook or Peary? Have a look at some of the evidence for and against each explorer.

ROBERT E PEARY

For:

- He was a very experienced Arctic explorer.
- He had nearly reached the North Pole before.
- He learnt vital survival skills from Inuit experts.
- He hand-picked the fastest dogs for his sleds.

Against:

- He couldn't have travelled at the speeds he claimed.
- His straight route back wasn't possible because of the drifting ice.
- He buried Cook's papers in the Arctic so they couldn't be checked.
- He refused to hand over his own expedition diary.